Build a Great Career

A Guide for New (and Veteran) Employees

Bill Ward

Table of Contents

Foreword

My main passion in life is healthy relationships. It's the topic of my blogs and my self-help book. That's probably why I wanted to devour this incredibly empowering book in one sitting. I didn't have that opportunity. Conversely, I was able to peruse the wealth of information at my leisure, which is a good thing. There is too much priceless information to take down notes. The entire work should be kept as a reference.

In fact, it should be required reading for every new hire. I cannot tell you how much trauma and drama would have been circumvented if such wisdom had been available at my places of work.

In the end, the true beauty of Mr. Ward's words is that they are not limited to the corporate environment. They translate well to any group: family, religious organization, club, small business, volunteer group, and so forth. It's all about teamwork, whatever (and wherever) that team may be.

Bravo, Mr. Ward! Thanks for showing us there's more strength in collaboration than in individuality!

Traci Lawrence

Author of Accept No Trash Talk: Overcoming the Odds

Preface

I have been a manager for several years, and I've benefitted from working with a wide variety of employees. I have developed leaders and helped them through many tough situations with their employees. Many of these issues could have been avoided if the employees had access to, and followed advice about what their bosses valued.

The gift of feedback can make all the difference in a person's career. Unfortunately, not everyone is lucky enough to receive the kind of pointers that can be leveraged to make important changes in conduct. This book will provide you with tips for analyzing the path you are currently on. You can also use it to assess whether you need to change some behaviors in order to build the kind of career you really want.

This allegory follows Henry Williams as he overcomes trouble in his new career. It captures the feedback he receives as he works to overcome his rough start. Henry is lucky to work at Powell, where he has the opportunity to learn from several senior executives. Ultimately, he is able to synthesize the advice he receives into a model that is applicable to each of us.

Acknowledgements

I appreciate the support of my good wife Lauril, the encouragement of Christine Sargent and Zac Palmer, and, the many employees I've had the opportunity to learn from over the years.

I also wish to thank my friend and Editor, Traci Lawrence.

Chapter 1: Orientation Day

Henry pulled into the parking lot on his first day at the new firm, Powell United. He noticed that his was certainly the oldest car in the lot; but, it was definitely not a classic. As he pressed the clutch to gear down, entering the parking lot, he realized that this was the beginning of being an adult. He'd worked hard in high school and college to earn the interview opportunity. Yet, the whole interview process was a hazy memory to him now.

He thought back to the interview day. He had arrived at headquarters thirty minutes early for the interview, worrying and sweating while he sat; first in the car, then in the lobby. While he sat waiting for his interview, he noticed the many people rushing in through the security gate only to disappear into the belly of the firm. At that time, he thought it would be great to be one of them.

As he brought himself back to reality, he locked his car and walked up to the security desk. This was where he would get his new badge and fill out his paperwork. He began to be excited about all the great things he was going to do for the company.

He had graduated near the top of his class and had always been looked to as a leader. He had achieved his Eagle Scout award at age 16. He had also been the president of his junior class in high school and an officer in his college fraternity. Henry had carefully taken every opportunity to polish his resume and build his reputation.

Lost in thought, he abruptly found himself at the security desk. Someone ahead of him had forgotten her badge, so they made small talk while the temporary badge was prepared. She was an attractive woman who looked professional in her business suit. She was confident and professional, but kind and generous with her laughter. She gave Henry her full attention while they spoke. Her name was Alice, or Margaret, or something. He couldn't remember for sure; but, he also realized it didn't really matter. He was able to get his badge, fill out his paperwork, and start his new employee onboarding program.

Henry's first day at Powell United was a rush of many rapidly introduced policies and programs. There were three more new guys in his cohort, and they seemed nice enough. They were all from good schools.

They seemed similar to him in many ways. The young men were a group of high achievers who had been spending their whole lives proving their worthiness. Finally, they had their chance to prove it in the workforce.

The Human Resources (HR) officer came into the room at some point during the day. He explained that the company had recently begun a mentoring program. New employees in certain roles would be assigned a senior team member to be their mentor starting with this hiring group. While Henry was generally interested in the mentoring program, he was far more interested in getting out of orientation and finally beginning the work he'd been hired to do. "Really," he thought, "a class on how to operate my e-mail?" Rather than cause a scene, he decided to go with the flow.

Over coffee during the break, he spoke to his new peers about how boring orientation is at Powell. "They think we don't know anything at all," he said. "Look, we're smart guys. We finished college and passed all the interviews to get to where we are; and, this guy is teaching us how to do e-mail?" The other men at the table nodded and laughed, but none said anything in response.

"And the guy they sent to us; is he for real? I can only guess he failed his normal job, so he has to do the orientations. Let's bring him some shampoo tomorrow," Henry continued. The uncomfortable looks on two of the other new employees were not registered by Henry, who was thinking of the next zinger.

At length, the break ended and the group returned to the onboarding room. Luke, another of the new employees, started an instant messaging conversation with Henry.

Every few minutes they exchanged criticisms and jokes about their situation. Some of the things Luke said made Henry uncomfortable at first, but he went along with it. Their friendship had begun.

On the third day of orientation Henry met Paul, who introduced himself to Henry as his direct supervisor. While the conversation was brief, Henry felt that Paul was someone who knew what he was doing. He seemed stern and direct, but polite. He explained that he'd been a front-line supervisor for many years. He felt his influence, and ability to help people in their careers, was greatest in his current role. Although he'd had several opportunities to take a step away from the front lines, he'd rejected them. Paul wanted to continue helping his team grow as individuals and develop their careers.

Paul showed Henry to his cubicle, gave him his phone number, corporate American Express card, business cards, and company cell phone. His face got serious, and he lowered his voice, as he gave him some advice: "Sometimes, in a group of new employees, friendships emerge that don't represent the values and behaviors that we embody here at Powell. While it is important to build a network of resources across the facility, the first several months are critical.

We expect you to focus your energy on observing and embracing the values you see demonstrated by our employees."

As Paul disappeared into the hallways that Powell seemed to be made of, Henry reflected on the relationship he and Luke had begun. "At least, it's something to think about", he said to himself, almost aloud. After thinking about it for a moment, Henry returned to the orientation room for the ethics training. He nodded to Luke and asked the group if they'd like to get together after work to see the game over chicken wings. The other two politely declined, but Luke agreed. They found their seats as the HR business partner was introduced to the group.

Chapter 2: Mentoring Program

Henry was now three months into the job, and the work was easy and rewarding. Henry found that he really enjoyed the team he was on. They were all at least eight years older than him and had worked at the firm an average of five years. In addition, some of them had job experience prior to coming to Powell. They were supportive of Henry and made sure he knew the business processes that made the office run. He felt there was quite a bit of red tape; he sometimes cut corners. However, the team seemed to appreciate and respect him, in spite of his being new.

One Tuesday morning, he was concerned the project he was managing had fallen behind. Henry didn't want to disappoint Paul, so he prematurely advanced a few activities to overcome the negative float that was accumulating.

He knew his behavior was technically not on the up and up, since the business process requires an independent peer validation of the completion of the activities. Still, he was able to complete it in the system; and, he was sure no one would discover his shortcut.

In the afternoon, Paul came to Henry's desk and asked for a few minutes of his time. As Henry followed Paul down the hall toward the HR department, every day of his brief career raced in front of his eyes. He felt a bead of sweat rolling down his spine. His face felt warm, and he knew it was scarlet. Henry tried to understand why he was heading to HR. He tried to build a story to explain whatever he was going to be forced to discuss. On the other hand, Paul's step was light and energetic.

Henry began to wonder if Paul enjoyed disciplining his team, or if this was a symptom that things weren't as they appeared. Cautiously, he began to mount the courage to begin some small talk. He asked Paul how his weekend had been, whether he'd been able to play golf, or go deep sea fishing; things he knew Paul enjoyed. Paul's responses were succinct and dismissive, but not curt or rude.

Finally, they arrived at the office of Alice Bergman. Paul excused himself as he introduced Henry to the sharply dressed woman. Henry noted she had an office with a view over the woods and pond that was part of the campus at Powell.

"She must have worked here for decades," he thought. He recognized she'd reached a position of considerable influence and appeared to be in her late 50s. Alice was fit and seemed more youthful than her chronological age. He admitted to himself that he was actually in awe of her.

As she reached her hand out to give him a firm handshake, she looked him right in the eye and greeted him by his full name. "Henry Williams, I'm Alice Bergman. We've been watching you, and I'm glad to finally meet you personally."

All of the fears Henry had felt as they'd started toward her office resurfaced as she said this. He wondered if his red face was betraying him. She offered to get him something to drink, and he asked for a bottle of cool water. He was grateful for the diversion as he tried to slow his heart rate. He adjusted his position in the oversized leather wingback chair. The worn black leather contrasted against the brown slacks he wore.

Alice returned to the desk and offered the water and a coaster to protect her walnut desk. She asked forgiveness for slipping off her shoes as she curled her legs up and sat on them in her plush leather chair. She leaned forward and rested her elbow on the desk, holding her chin in her hand. She ran the fingers of her other hand through her silver hair. Then, she tucked her hair behind her ear and adjusted her glasses.

She studied Henry for a moment. His red-framed glasses added a youthful studiousness to his handsome face. A few freckles across his cheeks and nose seemed to reflect the sparkle in his crystal blue eyes. His dark hair was short and well groomed.

She inhaled and began slowly and deliberately, "Henry, as you may remember from your orientation, we have a mentoring program at Powell. There are twelve advisors across our network and only nine mentoring candidates. We sit on a mentoring committee, and we've discussed the strengths and areas of opportunity for all of the candidates. We have spent a great deal of time and energy talking about you and your situation. You do not fit the traditional profile of our mentoring candidates. You demonstrate many qualities that we look for, but you have many areas needing improvement. Since you are in the most recent hiring group, and we've committed to provide guidance, I have stood up to be your mentor."

Henry felt a flood of emotions. He was relieved to realize he wasn't in trouble. On the other hand, he didn't like hearing that he wasn't performing as expected.

"Henry, are you listening?" she continued. "You and I will meet each month on the first Monday of the month in my office at 11:00 am. We will establish goals and track milestones. I will be brutally honest with you. I will drop into meetings and interview people you work with. This will help me to understand the areas in which you need development. What questions do you have right now?"

Henry struggled to regain his focus. He hadn't brought any paper or pen to this impromptu meeting. He didn't know what kinds of questions were appropriate to ask. He looked at his camel-colored wingtips as he considered what he might inquire.

Finally, he had the composure to speak. He felt self-conscious, since he'd just been told he wasn't quite performing up to the standard. Yet, he was able to make a statement: "I've been a winner all my life. I haven't ever been told I wasn't good enough, or that I had areas needing refinement."

He felt himself choke up a bit as he continued, "These things are hard for me to hear." Alice listened intently. Henry could tell her concern for him was genuine. She leaned forward and locked her gaze to his. He had her undivided attention and he realized it, which reassured him.

Knowing she was there for him, although she had been stern, gave him the confidence to continue. "I know I'm a good person, and I have a lot to add to this company. Please help me."

Alice sat up straight in her chair and offered him the first of many lessons:

I care about you, Henry, and that's why I'm willing to be your mentor. I'll be honest and direct because I care about you. Please let me tell you a story that shaped how I feel about feedback:

I once saw a man walking through the halls at the end of the day whose pants were unzipped. I didn't know the man very well, but I knew his name. I reached my hand out to shake with him so I could get close enough to tell him about his problem. He was a little embarrassed; but, he was grateful I cared enough to help him out.

As I stopped by my desk to grab my briefcase, my receptionist told me it was good I had done that for the man. She and some of her friends had noticed it around lunch time. I asked her why she hadn't told him. My friend said she was worried about embarrassing him.

Listen, Henry, she was worried about making him uncomfortable, so she let him walk around the halls all day--and attend board meetings--with his pants unzipped. How embarrassing, indeed!

Henry, I consider feedback to be a gift. I would not let you walk around here with your pants unzipped, or with a booger on your face. In the same way, I wouldn't allow you to develop, or continue, habits and behaviors that keep you from your potential.

Just as you wouldn't think of ignoring advice about your pants, only a fool would ignore the kind of tips that illuminate blind spots in his behavior.

Henry returned from the meeting with much on his mind. He was grateful to learn there was someone in the company besides Paul who was willing to provide support and help him build his career. He did have to admit his confidence was a bit shaken.

As Henry sat at his desk throughout the rest of the day, he kept himself looking busy. However, he was really thinking about how he'd feel if he learned, at the end of the day, that he had a booger on his face. How embarrassing that would be! He started to think about the equivalent of unzipped pants in career terms. What are the blind spots she was talking about?

When Luke came by to ask Henry if he wanted to go for a drink after work, he agreed. They went to Jerry's Pub. Henry began the conversation: "You aren't listening, Luke. She told me I have many areas to work on. I've been here three months!" Luke nodded as he tried to understand how to help his buddy.

"How bad is it that they assigned me to the Human Resources Director?" Henry said. "I know one thing, though: I won't cut any more corners, and I'll do what I can to fix what I've done."

Chapter 3: Henry's Presentation

The conference room was full. There was just one seat remaining when Henry rushed in as the meeting began. While the meeting facilitator was trying to welcome the group and get the meeting underway, Henry noisily handed his jump drive, and whispered filenames to, the administrative assistant. He was shuffling through the papers in his lap, and trying to find his presentation, when the facilitator turned to him and introduced the title of his presentation.

By then, the admin (administrative assistant) had found the file; Henry's slides were being projected on the screen. Henry turned to his neighbor to borrow a laser pointer. The delay in beginning his presentation was awkward. Many of his peers began laughing softly at his situation.

As Henry rose to begin his presentation, he cleared his throat and spoke. Henry was a good public speaker. He quickly found his rhythm and presented the data in his slides skillfully and convincingly.

"This opportunity," he said, "is going to differentiate us. The numbers make sense. We have the right people to execute the mission; and, this project perfectly fits our company motto: 'Be good and do good; but, if you have to choose, be good'."

He delivered a powerful case and persuaded the executives to invest in his project. The crowd actually applauded. Henry beamed throughout the rest of the meeting; and, he nearly strutted back to his desk after the meeting.

Soon Paul stopped by to congratulate him on his successful presentation. "Although you got off to a clumsy start, you really hit your stride and nailed the presentation. It's clear you really know your stuff, and you can sell. I'm glad to have you on this team. You add a lot of value. What did you think was the best part?" Paul smiled genuinely at Henry as he waited for his response.

"When I said, 'this is our time!' I felt the electricity in the room," Henry replied. Nodding, Paul let that comment hang in the air. "That was a magical moment," he agreed.

Paul asked, "If you could do it over, is there any part you would do differently?" After thinking for a moment, Henry said that he didn't know what he'd do differently. He felt it had gone perfectly.

Paul looked at his own hands for a moment while remembering details from some recent "Crucial Accountability" training. Should he confront the event, the pattern of events, or the impact they had on their relationship? He decided to talk about the pattern he'd seen emerging from Henry:

There is one thing I would mention for improvement: You came into the meeting at the very last moment and disrupted the meeting. You coordinated with the admin while John was trying to get the meeting underway. That was distracting; in fact, rude. I don't know if you heard the chuckling in the back. Some of the mid-level managers, my boss included, were having some fun at your expense.

It's not just today, Henry. I've noticed this kind of behavior for some time now.

Deadlines are important at Powell; but, your behavior doesn't demonstrate that you value that part of our mission. I know you are trying to build a good career here, and you have great potential. I mean, look at how you moved the executives! Still, you need to be better prepared so you don't stick out in less complimentary ways.

Hey, I care about you. I'm really happy about your performance in there. It really was great! As competent as you are right now, these little setbacks are like rough spots on a gem that we just need to polish as we go.

The exuberance Henry had felt immediately following the presentation and meeting were a little deflated. On the other hand, he recognized the truth in what Paul had just told him. He was aware of the expectation to have all materials to the admin at least 30 minutes prior to the meeting. In addition, he had heard Paul's boss laughing.

Henry committed to making the changes Paul mentioned as he watched his boss walk back to his office. "How is it that Paul has so much power to get me to realize what I need to do to be a better employee and a more effective professional?" he wondered.

Monday of the following week was Henry's mentoring session. As he walked to Alice's office, the words that had been ringing in his ears all weekend seemed to be getting louder and more oppressive. He was glad Paul expressed confidence in him. He knew he had started to question his worth.

Suddenly, he was at the door of Alice's office. This time he had known to bring pen and paper.

"Please, come in," he heard Alice say. When he walked in, he saw that she was putting the finishing touches on a document. She gave her admin some final information about its distribution. "Water?" she asked, reaching in her mini-fridge for a fruit juice for herself. Coaster and water in hand, Henry settled into his chair to begin the session.

"I saw your presentation last week," Alice said, "Quite inspiring. You have a gift." Henry was pleased to hear someone so respected give him such a warm compliment. However, his experience with Paul was still fresh in his mind. He said, "Thank you," but he was bracing himself for the "but" that was coming next. It didn't come.

"Henry, as we've discussed, the expectation for these sessions is for you to bring in one thing you'd like to work on. I will also convey one idea I think you should develop. We'll have a little chat that may uncover opportunities for me to guide you in your career at Powell. What have you brought today?"

In spite of Henry's normal ability to speak articulately, today he stammered a bit. He was trying to organize his thoughts on the fly. He hadn't remembered the requirement to highlight an area for improvement. Also, he wasn't ready to talk about the feedback he'd received from Paul.

"I think I need some tips for time management," he finally uttered. As a young professional, he had already started building a network of friends in the community. Furthermore, he had joined a gym and a club. He was filling up his life with what he thought was socially expected of someone in his position. These activities, along with his true passion of maintaining and expanding his saltwater aquarium, may have led Henry to overextend his schedule.

"What is important is seldom urgent and what is urgent is seldom important," Alice blurted out. As she did so, she turned and pointed out a portrait of Dwight Eisenhower. "He's the author of that quote. You may have heard about it from The 7 Habits of Highly Effective People, by Stephen R. Covey."

"If you make a two-by-two table like this," she said as she slid paper over to him, "and identify what activities in your life fit into these quadrants, you'll know how to prioritize them.   It's helped me tremendously."

	URGENT	NOT URGENT
IMPORTANT	Group 1: Urgent and Important	Group 2: Important but Not Urgent
NOT IMPORTANT	Group 3: Urgent but Not Important	Group 4: Neither Important or Urgent

Figure 1. Eisenhower's Important vs. urgent matrix

Henry did appreciate the help. He realized that he accomplished some tasks because of feeling pressured, not because he enjoyed them. He looked at the paper for a moment, already thinking about what things in his life he'd eliminate. He knew the weekly poker game would have to go.

He and Alice spent some time talking about how one practically uses the rubric to carefully analyze their activities. This ensures people spend their most important resource, time, on the things that matter most.

As the discussion wound down, Alice looked at him pensively. Henry could tell she had something more for him.

"Now, I do have something prepared for you today, Henry." Alice began, as if on a mission. It seemed to Henry that he'd better brace himself because he knew Alice to be direct and candid.

"Henry," she began, "you are not neutral." He sat quietly studying the portrait of Eisenhower that he'd just been shown while he tried to understand what she had just said. The brief silence in the room was uncomfortable for him; he realized she was looking right into his eyes.

His facial expression must have revealed what his mind was thinking, so she continued to explain:

"The first time I met you, I began to piece together a puzzle of who I thought you were. Do you remember the first time we met? I had forgotten my badge at home and was getting a temporary badge for the day. You told me it was your first day on the job. You were worried about getting a real hard nose as a boss. Do you remember this?" she asked. He had to admit he didn't remember anything about the exchange.

Alice went on, "You have developed a reputation here as someone who is gifted, but isn't fully invested. Had you known that?"

Again, Henry's face was flush. It was uncomfortable to be faced with unflattering information. He didn't realize he was viewed that way; and, he didn't think it was an accurate depiction. He quietly replied, "I didn't know. I'm not sure what that really means."

"Once a cross-functional project is started, we often look through our lists of high performers to decide who should participate," Alice began. "When your name comes up, it usually sounds like this: 'We'd like Henry on our team, if we knew he'd do what was needed. He seems to still be deciding if he wants to be here, or if he's just here while watching for something better to come along.'

Alice inquired, "How does it feel to hear how people feel about you?" Henry sipped his water while grasping for the words to say. He didn't like thinking he had developed such a reputation in just five months of a new career.

He had always been given such positive feedback for every role he'd played. This was the first time he'd heard criticism like this. "What are the things I'm doing that give people this impression?" he was able to muster.

I'm glad you asked, Henry. I'm also glad you're open and not defensive. Often, when people hear feedback like this, the first inclination is to protest and try to explain why the opinion is false. Before we talk about what to stop, start, and continue doing, let's spend another minute talking about the impact of your reputation: Think about a pendulum at rest, hanging straight down. It's neither hanging to the right, nor to the left. It's neutral. Even when the pendulum swings normally, its average is still neutral … until it isn't. In your case, you aren't neutral anymore.

Of course, it's a metaphor for your reputation. At first, people don't know what to expect; you are neutral to them. Over time, people have certain expectations based on your interactions with them. Pretty soon you have a reputation.

Once you have developed a reputation, people will always be watching for evidence that their assessment of you is correct. It's possible to change your habits and behaviors for 100 days. Then again, the one interaction that reminds them of the old you will convince people they were right all along.

In other words, you'll have to work hard to convince people you have changed and that you're worthy of a new reputation. Does that make sense?

Henry sat quietly. He was thinking about how excited he'd been when he first joined the firm. Also, he wondered how it had all gone so wrong. Maybe he should quit and start over at a new firm. Maybe he should...

"Henry, I want you to know that I've helped many people in your situation, and I've had to do some of this type of reevaluation in my own career," Alice said, interrupting his thoughts. "Now let's talk about the steps to recover from this reputation."

They talked for some time. She gave him some practical steps to take. He'd jotted down helpful notes. His mind was full of the useful advice he'd received.

Henry returned home in a thoughtful state. He spent a lot of time thinking about the reputation building he needed to do. He also considered how he might streamline his life using the "important versus urgent" criteria he'd learned.

He picked up takeout from the Thai Palace and set himself up at the dinner table with a legal pad, his planner, and a pencil. He listed all his activities on the pad by looking at his planner and trying to remember ad hoc events from the last five weeks. After he completed the list, he categorized all of them as either important or urgent.

At length, Henry determined that he would abandon everything that was neither important nor urgent. He called his friends and told them he'd have to stop going to poker and to the Tuesday night basketball scrimmages. He'd reduce the Sports Center parties he was hosting to one per week. In addition, he'd quit one of his tropical fish clubs.

He also identified things important enough to continue investing his energy in. His continuing education program would pay dividends. He'd keep that in his life for sure. He would also continue, and maybe even increase, his reading routine. This would keep his mind sharp and further his interests.

The exercise was helpful, much like building a budget. It helped him to see on paper where he was spending his time, and how well his values aligned with his activities. He hoped these changes would ease some of his stress from keeping so many balls in the air.

Chapter 4: The Blowout

"Did you hear about Luke?" Henry overheard as he walked through the lobby. As he grabbed a drink in the break room on the way to his desk he heard others chatting as well. "He did not call him that...," one of the voices said. "Yes he did, and he said it loud," said another.

As far as Henry understood, his friend Luke had an argument with his department manager in front of the whole department. Evidently he'd been under some stress and had some concerns about the direction of the firm. It didn't help that he couldn't understand the vision of the manager.

Luke made a comment that could only be heard by a few people near him. However, Steve, Luke's department manager, noticed the commotion when they laughed. The supervisor quickly zeroed in on Luke, who repeated what he'd said. They began to exchange words. Luke didn't even know how or why he'd become so angry. He hadn't meant to say what he'd said; but, the damage was done.

Luke was sitting nervously at his desk waiting for something to happen when Henry came around to console his friend. "I heard a little bit about what happened, Luke. Are you doing ok? What can I do to help you?" Henry asked.

Luke didn't really feel like talking, although he was glad to see a friendly face. "I don't know what came over me, but I think I'm done here," Luke said without looking up at his friend.

Henry had learned a lot from the reputation-improvement sessions with Alice, so he offered some tips: "Look, Luke, it's probably not as bad as you think. These things pass; but, you'll have to work hard to overcome what you've done."

He tried to console his buddy; yet, the timing didn't seem right. He knew how it felt to be in the immediate aftermath of an event like this. Luke wasn't really in the mood to be with people, so Henry patted him on the shoulder and reminded him that he was there for him.

As Henry walked to his own desk, he thought about the situation and what Alice might recommend. She really had helped him over the last four months. The letters, AARP, was a nice way to remember what she'd taught him. He reflected on what he'd written in his notes:

- Accept that the information you are hearing is valid. It may not be fully accurate, but there must be some basis in truth--even if it's only someone's perspective. Your job is to accept that it is your job to fix it.

- **A**ssess what information you have been provided. How can you make use of the knowledge? Speak with other people you work with for a thorough understanding. They will make you aware of what led them to certain conclusions.

- **R**eject the habits of your old reputation. List them if you must to remind you of the practices you need to avoid. Daily reminders help keep you on task.

- **P**rotect the reputation you are trying to build. Focus your energy on the things you want to be known for. Practice the habits which, over time, will ensure your new reputation.

He had finally been asked to be on the cross-functional team formed to study the design of the new education outreach program. Alice had called in a favor to get him on the team, but he didn't mind. He just needed a chance to show he was fully engaged.

At Henry's next mentoring meeting with Alice, he was ready for his topic to come up. Instead of talking about what he wanted to improve, he wanted to get Alice's perspective on Luke's situation. Luke had received a written warning, but didn't seem to be at risk of losing his job.

Alice started up, "I'm actually quite glad you brought that up today. What kind of opportunities do you think Luke has closed for himself?"

Henry thought about it for a moment. "I don't think Steve will go out on a limb for him. Maybe he won't get as many big projects to work on," he offered.

Alice nodded thoughtfully. She had a graceful way about her--an elegance that seemed to add to her credibility. She started speaking slowly, "This is the kind of thing I wouldn't normally talk about, but I'm starting to see some real potential in you, Henry. Please keep this between us: Luke has surrendered a lot by his behavior. Maybe you don't know, but the reason the disagreement escalated so quickly is because Steve and Luke have a history of throwing barbs at each other.

"It started in fun," she continued. "Then, the zingers grew more personal and hurtful in nature. Steve confided in me that he didn't really like having Luke on his team. When the facilities department was looking for a new analyst, Steve offered up Luke. No one would have him. He had more than a bad reputation; he had offended several people across the site."

I heard, in fact, that you've stopped getting together with him after work. Why is that?" she asked patiently.

Henry adjusted himself uneasily in his chair, "I didn't like how he spoke to the waitresses. I didn't want to feel like he was representing me when we were together." Henry said, finally resuming eye contact.

"That's just it," she said, a little louder than either of them expected. "That's exactly how Steve feels about him. He's a member of the team, but Steve doesn't appreciate the way Luke represents him."

"In crude terms, this is a good example of the phrase, 'Don't crap where you eat,'" she continued. "I've known Steve for years. Between you and me, Luke will have a hard time overcoming this. It's such an important concept. There are so many ways one can crap where they eat. All of them represent an act which stands in the way of careers, or desires."

Henry thought about this concept over the next several weeks. He wondered about some of the incidents he'd seen. He also considered whether they were the type of situations to which Alice had been referring.

He remembered a football player in college who destroyed his professional football chances because he'd been arrested at a fraternity party. The athlete protested his innocence. However, in the end it didn't matter if he was guilty or not. He'd been involved, and that presented too much of a risk for any agent.

There was also the time he saw a high school teacher getting too friendly with some of her students. She was forced to resign from her job. Henry remembered hearing that she had a hard time finding another teaching job. He resolved to be aware of his actions and behavior to avoid sabotaging his own career.

Chapter 5: Promotion Plan

Henry drove to work in his new BMW Z4. Actually, it was a two-year-old model; but, it was new to him. He'd done well at Powell, so he treated himself for his work anniversary. The car was perfect to drive in the spring sunshine. He put down the top and went to work the long way. He felt happy.

His mind reviewed the last year. He'd learned quite a bit about the business and about how to get work done. He was grateful for the mentoring he'd received from Alice. Henry was also grateful for the keys to success she'd led him to. He was sad to see Luke leave the company; although, he'd landed on his feet in a company that runs coffee restaurants.

He pulled his car into the furthest parking spot in the lot. He enjoyed the walk from the lot to the lobby. He walked with a bounce in his step, thinking about the bright future he had in store at Powell.

He saw Shane walking up to the lobby at the same time. Shane and Henry had worked together on a project to market a product for preteens. They had been successful and had enjoyed working together. They occasionally had lunch together.

Today, Shane was beaming. "What's up, Bud? You look like you are on top of the world," Henry said, holding open the door to the lobby for Shane. "I am," Shane responded. "I just learned that my promotion went through!"

Shane had been at the firm for almost five years. He was being promoted to level 2. It came with an 8% pay increase. In addition, he would now be eligible to work on bigger international projects and attend Powell's leadership institute. They had been trying to mimic some of the leadership programs at larger firms and integrating a visiting speaker series.

As Henry heard about the perks, he started to consider how a promotion would create opportunities for building his career. He patted Shane on the shoulder, congratulated him, and wished him a pleasant day.

Paul was stirring creamer into his coffee in the break room as Henry walked by. Henry was deep in thought, and he didn't notice Paul was even there. He was wondering what was necessary to be ready for a promotion when the time came.

He knew he'd started at the firm with some weaknesses. On the other hand, he also knew he'd won the respect of Paul and Alice. He was aware that he had the tools and skills he needed to go far.

"But, what do I do?" he asked himself, almost aloud. In his year at Powell, he had never heard anyone talk about how promotions are earned. He spent hours looking at Powell's intranet to see if there was anything that would help him know how to prepare himself. He couldn't find anything at all.

He started asking a few of his peers if they knew how promotions are earned. None of them could help him. They seemed to believe it was a mystery. Finally, he determined to consult five different experienced managers. He'd keep a journal of their advice.

"Henry, what's on your mind?" Paul called down the hall. "You seem so deep in thought. Is everything ok? How was your weekend?"

"Oh, my weekend was great. I bought a car for myself. I spent all day Sunday driving through the woods with the top down. It was really great," he replied.

"Then why the thoughtful look?" Paul asked again. Henry started slowly, "On my way in today I ran into Shane. We've become friends since we worked together on that project last fall. He's a great guy, and I've learned a lot from him." Henry continued, "I just learned that he got promoted to Level 2. Honestly, I'm really happy for him."

Henry rubbed his forehead with the back of his hand and his eyes finally met Paul's. "It just made me think about what I should be doing to ensure I'll be ready for Level 2 when the time comes. Let me ask you what you think of this idea: I think what I'd like to do is interview five experienced managers at the firm to get advice, keep their responses in a journal, then work with you on how to implement the things I've learned. Does that seem like a good plan?"

Paul cleared his throat. He offered a raspberry jelly filled pastry to Henry, inviting him to Paul's office. As they walked to the office, Paul started to explain: "When you first started here, we considered putting you into the emerging leaders program. Once we saw some of your habits, we felt the time wasn't right yet. Frankly, you have overcome the reputation you formed here originally. I have been pleased with your ability to learn from feedback."

"Have a seat," he said as they entered Paul's office and shut the door behind them. Both of the men seated themselves at the desk.

"Let me give you a coaster for your coffee," Paul said as he extended his arm toward him with a familiar coaster. "I'll support your plan. In fact, it's a fairly good idea to select several people to interview in order to get different perspectives. The only condition I'd put on it is that you let me and Alice be part of your five."

Paul continued, "I'd also like to give you a couple of tips for your interviews: Ask them what traits have most helped them and what characteristics they've noticed in the most promising associates. Let's not drag this on, Henry. I'd like to see your list by Wednesday. Let's try to have the meetings completed by the end of the month. Does that seem achievable?"

Henry thought about who he would put on his list. Now that Alice and Paul were on the list, he only needed three more. He spoke quietly, "If I put someone on my list that I don't know, are you able to introduce me?" Henry asked timidly.

Paul nodded confidently, "There are only a few people I couldn't introduce you to, but Alice might be able to help. I would recommend that you don't go too high on the organization chart. Many of the executives don't like to spend too much time with the new associates. In contrast, there are a few who realize that investments in our associates will keep our company strong for the future."

Overnight, Henry thought more about who he'd put on his list. Janet, Shane's boss, had been the sponsor of the project they'd worked on together. She seemed to like Henry. She was an A-type personality who was driven and direct about what she expected from her employees and the projects she sponsored. Henry wasn't sure she was the right one. However, she had gone to bat for Shane to get him his promotion.

As Henry ate his breakfast before leaving for work, he heard an interview on the radio with Angela Duckworth. Her work in psychology focuses on a topic she calls "grit". She defines the trait as "sticking with things over the very long term until you master them." (Hanford, 2012) She'd noticed while teaching middle school math that the students who gave the most effort did the best. The data was independent of intelligence quotient (IQ) or other advantages. She came to believe that this willingness to work hard is the key differentiator for success. She developed what she called the Grit Test, and she has been able to test her theories in various settings.

Persistent people have proven to be far more successful than those possessing any other attribute in the following areas: at West Point, an elite Military Academy in the US; among Scripps spelling contestants in the US; and, at various academic institutions. Henry started to wonder if he was tenacious enough. He didn't know.

While he was considering it, he heard Duckworth say, "It turns out a personality trait like extroversion can change a lot over a person's life. If you look at large population data, people get more or less extroverted over time," said Duckworth. "There's no reason to think that grit is any different." (Hanford, 2012) Perhaps even if Henry didn't possess these traits now, he may be able to develop them.

Henry spent the rest of the morning considering what he'd heard. As a result, he was almost late for work. He decided that, rather than looking for who he'd pick to fill the rest of his list, today he'd look for signs of grit among the people he worked with. It was going to be an interesting day.

Chapter 6: The Interview Group

Henry finally had his list of five. He had spoken of it with Alice, and she agreed with his list. Alongside Paul and Alice Henry had put Maria, Dereck and Lucas. Maria was a manager in human resources. She facilitated the emerging leaders program for the company. Dereck was a department manager who had been on the promotion board for many years. Lucas was a recent transfer to the complex where Henry worked. He was the youngest Senior Associate in the region.

Henry felt like these three could provide the additional advice to supplement what he'd learn from Alice and Paul. He had even arranged for them all to meet together after the interviews so that Henry could present his findings to the group. Maria even felt his report might be useful for improving the emerging leaders program.

Chapter 7: Showing Up

"Showing up," Dereck explained as their conversation began. "That's the essential activity. You must show up. It may not make sense until I explain it to you. I guess the other thing I'd add is lead where you stand."

Henry was situating the now familiar coaster while he listened and struggled to comprehend what Dereck was saying. "Are you telling me to be to work on time?" Henry asked. "That doesn't seem to be so hard. It seems like, how do you call it, the price of entry."

Slowly shaking his head while stirring some creamer into his coffee, Dereck responded, "Let me explain by telling you a story: I'd been at Powell about two years when I was asked to start attending a daily quality meeting. At first, I went grudgingly. I didn't see any value in attending, but I did as my supervisor requested. I never spoke unless I needed to represent my department on some topic. One day, on the way out of the meeting, the sponsor of the meeting asked me to follow him to his office."

Dereck continued, "He asked me why I thought I was in the meeting. I told him that every department needed to be represented, and I was chosen for my department. He asked me why I had been chosen. I had to admit I didn't know. Then, the manager explained to me that, although I was present at the meeting, I wasn't really engaged. He told me I'd been selected because I possessed certain abilities that were needed to make this meeting useful. I hadn't shown up with my strengths".

Dereck was easy to listen to. He had a smooth baritone voice that was soothing without causing drowsiness. He spent some time explaining to Henry what happened after he'd become fully engaged. The group began to have serious success. "So you see," Dereck concluded, "by showing up in that meeting, fully and consistently, our group was able to develop trust. We learned to confront problems and develop innovative programs and improvements."

"Wow!" Henry accidentally gasped aloud. He knew that he was in some recurring meetings where he hadn't really "shown up". He quickly wrote in his career journal. The silence was comfortable between the men.

"One more question, if you don't mind: What did you mean by 'Lead where you stand'?" Henry said, as he sipped his coffee.

"Ah, yes," Dereck said, wiping the last crumbs of donut from the corner of his mouth.

"Once I started feeling what it was like to work in such a successful cross-functional team, I began to crave the opportunity to continue increasing my influence. I used to look for opportunities to lead teams. I think I even began to become a nuisance to some of the managers who sponsored them."

Dereck went on, "Finally, in frustration over my continued pressure to choose me to lead her team, one of the managers exclaimed that I should lead where I stand. 'I'll choose you to be the team lead when I'm confident that you can lead from within the team,' she'd said. 'Lead where you stand!' This advice has made all the difference in my career. Show up and be a leader from wherever you are in the group."

Chapter 8: Be Competitive

A few days later, Henry brought two sodas to Lucas' office thinking it would be nice to treat him for his generosity. When he arrived at Lucas' office, he noticed that he was alone. "Lucas must be running a little late," Henry thought to himself. He let himself into the office and got two cups and two coasters. He put one out for each of them and sat, looking at the certificates on the wall of the office.

Lucas had been recognized for some pretty impressive accomplishments. His bachelors, masters and JD degree certificates all hung in a cluster on the wall. He'd been all over the country getting his education: UCLA for International Relations; Clemson for a Masters in Accounting; and, Harvard Law to finish it up. Lucas had also been recognized by the Austin Chamber of Commerce for running one of their events while working in Powell's Austin office.

Lucas was an athletic man with bronze skin. His perfect white teeth shone when he smiled, and he was always smiling. "Henry, please excuse me for being late," Lucas said as he whirled into the room, grabbing Henry's outstretched hand in both of his. "I'm sorry to have wasted your time. Is this soda for me? Why, thank you Henry. You are so thoughtful." Lucas plopped himself into his high-back leather chair. "You used a coaster, too; how considerate. Thank you, Henry!"

"Tell me, Henry," Lucas began, "were you the valedictorian at your high school?" Henry looked at his thumbs rubbing together nervously. "Not the valedictorian, but I was in the top five out of 452 in my class," he said as he wondered where this was going.

A soft chuckle emerged from Lucas' bulky chest as he looked into Henry's eyes. "How about college? Where did you finish in college?" he asked with a twinkle in his eye.

"Top one percent," Henry said with a little more pride. "And I earned it. I gave up a lot to have such good grades. I wouldn't go to many sporting events, dances, or even eat lunch with other people. I only joined the fraternity because I knew I could learn a lot by engaging in the leadership aspects..."

"Easy now," Lucas broke in. "I know your history. I know you've worked hard to get where you are. You have generally been the smartest person in any group you've found yourself in. I know you've pushed yourself; but, things have usually come easier for you than for most. Am I right?"

Henry wasn't sure where this was going. He listened carefully and watched as Lucas inhaled deeply and began, "You have risen to the top throughout your life. You have developed a level of confidence that is appropriate for someone of your intellect; confidence that borders on arrogance," Lucas said, tapping his glasses.

"You have pushed yourself; yet, you have always known success," he continued. "When you came to Powell, you joined a group that was more at your level than the people you've tended to interact with. While your confidence is natural, it butts up against those that represent natural competition."

Lucas rose and walked around the desk and sat on the edge of the desk, just inches away from Henry. He rested his hand on Henry's arm. "Henry you've got to compete here if you want to rise to the top. This team is intelligent. While some have lost much of their fire to compete, they should not be underestimated. You need to do what you can to differentiate yourself; not as an equal team member, but as one who can be turned to as the go-to guy. You must excel to the point that your peers know of your skills and talents. Also, you want your accomplishments to become known to management."

Henry shrugged off Lucas' touch. "I was always told that your work should speak for itself. 'If you have to toot your own horn, the tune isn't very sweet.'" Henry was actually quite confused now. He knew he could do more and work harder, but bragging about his work just didn't make sense to him.

"Let me clarify," Lucas said as he walked over to a plush wing back chair whose dark leather surface nearly matched his hair. "There is a difference between boasting about every detail of your work and ensuring those who care about an issue or project realize you are the one making it happen. In fact, I sometimes choose projects to work on based on which executive is invested in the project. I'm just doing the best I can to see to it that the project runs well. I might be the one to send the meeting minutes, or to provide status updates to the executive team."

Lucas continued, "It's not about stealing the spotlight. It's about demonstrating that you realize the same things are important as the management team does. Does that make it any clearer?" Henry had to admit this was going to take some time to sink in, but he was willing to be open to the idea.

The time was about up, and Henry didn't want to leave without asking any questions. "How will I know when I've reached the right balance?" Something in Lucas' look told him he'd have to figure that out on his own.

As Henry drove his Z4 through the park on his way home, he pulled off the road to see if he could think in the cool night air. He reached into his computer bag and slid out his career journal so he could review the notes. "How can I let the work I'm doing get more visibility?" he thought. He sat on the trunk of his car, trying to think of examples he'd seen among his peers. "I may as well try", he concluded.

Chapter 9: Represent Appropriately

Alice was interested in how Henry's interviews were going. She had been on vacation, so they hadn't met in a month. However, she'd thought a lot about the promise Henry was starting to show. She opened up a fruit juice as she reviewed the notes she'd been keeping on their meetings. As she ran her finger down the notes, her eye caught hold of a heavily traced and underlined word on the page: REPRESENT!

Just as she'd come to that word, Henry knocked lightly and entered the office. "How good to see you," he said. "How was your vacation? What was the most fun thing you did?" After some small talk about Alice's visit to her daughter's home to see her grandsons, they got down to business.

Alice asked suddenly, "Henry, what does it mean to represent Powell?" It was a bit abrupt. However, since Henry trusted Alice would only try to help him, he didn't feel worried about what was next.

"I remember that Powell values things like global leadership, community involvement, and environmental consciousness."

"That's not what I mean," Alice said patiently. "As an associate at Powell, you are known in the community. The things you do are a reflection on us. You represent the company, and you represent Paul within the company. I wanted to tell you about something that happened on my vacation: I went with my daughter and her sons to breakfast at a Phoenix restaurant. The kids were excited because we were planning to get tropical fish after breakfast."

She knew of Henry's tropical fish hobby, but continued without mentioning it. "They had a hard time keeping their excitement down and weren't behaving very well at the restaurant. My daughter was doing what she could to control the boys. As the waitress came over, she explained to me that her own grandsons were little princes and that something must be wrong with these kids."

A tear welled up in Alice's eyes as she continued, "The waitress judged me based on the actions of my grandsons. While I understand that boys will be boys and some days are better than others, I thought a lot about how the boys represented their mother and me."

There was a long silence as both Alice and Henry thought about the situation and how it characterized the workplace.

Henry nodded thoughtfully and wrote a few notes in his career journal.

Soon their eyes met. Alice offered her hand to Henry and he knew he was being excused. "I'm looking forward to your presentation in two weeks," she said, as Henry stepped over the threshold of her office door and disappeared down the hall.

Chapter 10: Customer Service

Maria had a warm smile as she welcomed Henry into her office. It was a large office that had a conference table and a video conference monitor. Honestly, it was an impressive office. Henry set out two coasters as he poured them each a glass of lemonade he'd brought to share. Maria finished putting away a few files that were laying on her desk and arranged her pens to the left of her mouse pad. She arranged them by color as they appear in the rainbow. "She has a little obsessive-compulsive disorder (OCD)," Henry thought to himself. He realized he shouldn't make a joke about it.

He explained that he'd been a mentee to Alice; coached by Lucas and Dereck; and. he was working with Paul to see how he could build his career. "I have to say I've learned a lot. I've had to challenge some of what I'd thought was conventional wisdom about building a career."

Henry was proud of what he'd learned in the past several weeks. He showed Maria his career journal. He'd filled up more than twenty pages with notes and thoughts. He was grateful Paul had put him on this path.

"Who is your customer?" Maria asked, softly but with purpose. "Oh, we have clients all over the world," he replied. "Right now I'm working on a project that the government intends to send to Australia and I…"

"No, that's not what I mean," Maria interrupted. "Do you have any internal customers? Who are the people whose success relies on you doing your job right?"

She stood to look out the window at the pond below in order to give Henry a moment to think. Powell had built the pond years ago to demonstrate their commitment to the environment and the local swan population.

"Paul is a customer because I represent him and Powell." Henry was actually proud of that answer. He'd already been advised twice by Alice about the importance of representing the firm and your manager well.

Maria kindly solicited, "And who else?" She'd said it without even turning to look at him. "I guess Jerry from accounting needs to have my reports on time in order to finish his work each week. I know that sometimes, when I'm a day late, he sure gets tense. And then there is the lady from the print shop. I noticed that, when I give her an extra day or two for a large job, she is far more tolerant of mistakes or customization. She might be my customer, too," Henry said.

Maria slowly turned from the window. Henry noticed how the light passing through her hair made it seem to glow. "Yes," she said lifting the lemonade cup to her lips and taking a sip. "That is correct. Everyone that works at Powell is your customer: contractors, executives, coffee shop workers, and custodial crew. Remembering this can help you in your career. Do you know that I once saw Mr. Powell sitting at lunch with the ladies from the mailroom? Mr. Powell recognized that everyone at this, and every Powell facility, was adding value to the mission and deserved his respect. His legacy lives at Powell as we all carry on in his footsteps."

"Every person in every office, working on every project, is interdependent," Maria continued. "We need each other. Our organization is intentionally organized so that none of us succeeds independently of the other functional groups. We really do need each other." She stopped to study Henry as he wrote in his career journal.

Henry actually hummed as he wrote, as if he were finishing the calculus of this new tip. "If everyone is my customer, then, I'm also a customer to many of the people at Powell. My projects are as important to them as their projects need to be to me. If I am to succeed, I need to build a network of support and resources across the company; especially at this facility," Henry thought as he finalized the organization of his thoughts.

Maria's voice broke his contemplation, "We call it COLLABORATION, and we look for it from every individual. It is an essential skill at Powell. Without it, you really can't succeed here."

Henry finished capturing his thoughts in the book and stood to leave. He expressed his gratitude for the help and for the time she'd given him. As Henry made his way back up to his desk, he began to see people differently. He saw them as resources, partners, and customers. When he viewed the relationships in this way, he felt a greater sense of obligation to collaborate and support the needs of others.

Chapter 11: Daring Greatly

Henry was feeling enthusiastic about all the new information he'd learned. He knew he was going to be a better employee. He was sure grateful for all the mentors he'd met who had taken precious time to help him. As he looked through his notebook, he saw that he had one more mentoring session planned. He had deliberately left Paul for last. He wanted to impress Paul with what he'd learned so far.

He went to the calendar on his computer to schedule the meeting and noticed a calendar request from Maria. The meeting's subject said "career development workshop". He didn't have much time, but it seemed important enough to stop and read the contents of the message:

"Henry, I really enjoyed the time we spent together last week. I've been thinking about how the notes in your journal might provide some benefit for other people to improve their careers. While it would definitely help each person, the sum of these improvements would be very helpful to Powell in meeting our objectives."

Henry saw now that he was going to have to skip grabbing a coffee on his way to the next meeting. "Please prepare a few slides about your findings to share with the executive committee next Friday," Henry read. He stood to leave his desk, overwhelmed by the magnitude of this request.

Next, he was off to see Paul at his desk. "I've wondered about these coasters I keep seeing in some people's offices," Henry said to Paul as they sat. Henry placed his coaster in front of himself on the desk and placed a bottled water on it.

Paul picked one of the coasters up, and rolled it across his palm, as he started to speak: "These coasters were designed by Mr. Powell himself. He visited Germany as a young man. He saved the coasters from twenty-nine cafes and beerhouses across the Bavarian region. Something about them had stuck with him. The rumor is that he decorated his den with some framed coasters. To Mr. Powell, the coaster represented the courtesy that his company should always show when working for a client.

His wish was that, like a coaster, his company would represent protection of its assets and the Powell professional brand. They are intended to remind all employees to think about the little things when caring for the client.

Having this coaster reminds me to align my goals and behaviors with the goals and mission of the company."

Paul set down the coaster and placed his coffee on it in front of him. The supervisor let the silence hang in the air as he seemed to think about something off in the distance. "That is also why you often see quotes and pictures of the people being quoted in offices around here," Paul said.

Henry remembered that he had seen several pictures of famous people with their quotes. One by Dwight Eisenhower hung in Alice's office. A saying by the Wright Brothers was displayed in one of the conference rooms.

Henry cleared his throat and began to speak. Not sure quite where to begin, he scratched his right eyebrow nervously. "Right before I came over here, I noticed Maria sent me a meeting request. It sounds like she wants to hear the results of my interviews. Do you know anything about this?" Henry looked right into Paul's eyes. There was no aggression. Instead, there was an expression of longing to understand.

Paul tapped his pencil on the table as he began to respond: "Maria is impressed with what you are doing, and she feels like it's the kind of thing that all people can benefit from. The problem is that, while the interviews are extremely valuable in many ways, the time commitment from upper managers isn't sustainable. She wants to find a way to make your experience portable so that others may benefit from it."

Henry was still confused by the request, and Paul could see it in his facial expression. "Powell has been successful and has continued to grow over the years. You have hit on something unique here. In order for us to be as strong as we need to be, we want our associates to grow as fast as they can. We take a bit of a chance when we hire a new associate because we only have so much information to go on when we commit to them."

"We've already talked about some of the misgivings we had when we brought you onboard. However, we've also been pleased to see how you've accepted and incorporated this feedback," Paul said. "The belief among the executive committee is that if folks could begin their career with the same guidance and mentoring you've received, we might be able to accelerate the process of getting our associates up to the level where they begin to really add value." Henry was blushing because he didn't realize that his little experiment had gained the attention of anyone at all.

"Paul, you are my last interview for the project," Henry began. "I wanted to be sure I gave you a chance to give your advice before we run out of time. I'm ready to write," he said.

"Ok, thank you," Paul said. "One of the things I want to share comes from a book I've just read. Brene' Brown wrote a book called Daring Greatly. She studies something she calls wholeheartedness. She encourages us to embrace vulnerability and imperfection, to live wholeheartedly, and to courageously engage in our lives."

Henry wrote as he responded. "That sounds a lot like the "showing up" that Dereck told me about." Paul inched himself to the front of his seat as he responded: "It is. But, it's more. It includes embracing vulnerability in our lives and acting anyway. The fact that we are not guaranteed success, yet there are things worth doing anyway, drives our need to dare greatly."

Henry interrupted, "Does it have anything to do with that quote you have on your wall?" He stood to read it:

The Man in the Arena by Theodore Roosevelt

"It is not the critic who counts; not the man who points out how the strong man stumbles, or where the doer of deeds could have done them better. The credit belongs to the man who is actually in the arena, whose face is marred by dust and sweat and blood; who strives valiantly; who errs, who comes short again and again, because there is no effort without error and shortcoming; but who does actually strive to do the deeds; who knows great enthusiasms, the great devotions; who spends himself in a worthy cause; who at the best knows in the end the triumph of high achievement, and who at the worst, if he fails, at least fails while daring greatly, so that his place shall never be with those cold and timid souls who neither know victory nor defeat." (Roosevelts, 1910)

"Wow, this is great!" Henry said as he stood staring at the portrait of the Rough Rider, Theodore Roosevelt. He was moved by the sentiment and realized that Paul was right. It was more than just showing up.

"I could listen to that poem every day," Paul said. "It has given me courage when I've needed it more than once. Another thing that goes with living this way is that sometimes we fail." Paul stood and walked over to sit on his window sill. Looking out the window at the parking lot he said wistfully, "Yes, sometimes we fail..."

Paul let his voice trail off before he caught himself. "The key to success is in how we handle disappointments. For every successful associate here at Powell, there are almost as many disappointments as there are victories. The character of a person can be best identified in those moments when things haven't gone as they wished. So that's my advice for you Henry: show up, be vulnerable, take chances, and overcome disappointment."

Henry frantically wrote down his thoughts as Paul tidied up his table in preparation to leave for his next meeting. "So sorry, I've taken too much time; now I have to run," Paul apologized.

Henry continued writing even after Henry had left. He sat in amazement at what he'd heard and, more surprisingly, about how he felt. Perhaps this was the secret.

At length, Henry was on his way back to his cubicle. However, he didn't notice any of the other associates as he made his way back through the maze of hallways.

He snuck a peak at some of Brene' Brown's work on his phone later in the break room. He was so surprised at the insight Paul had shared that he had to go to its source. Brene's way of talking about doing things that scare you penetrated into his mind and heart. Furthermore, he considered how this might be implemented in his own daily work.

Chapter 12: The Executive Committee Presentation

Henry woke early on Wednesday morning. This was going to be an important day. He'd been preparing his presentation for Maria. He learned that all of the people he'd interviewed were going to be there, so he was a little nervous. He wanted to ensure that he rendered what they had shared in a way that was truthful and unvarnished. He reviewed his PowerPoint slides several times throughout the morning and over lunch.

At length, the final edits were completed. Henry submitted the file to the admin for what he would come to realize was the executive committee meeting. It wasn't just Maria, Alice, Dereck, Paul and Marcus. It was also the site director, the finance director, and the corporate HR director.

He seated himself quietly at the front of the room at the boardroom table. He recognized everyone in the room, but hadn't met all of them until now.

He clung to his bottle of water on the familiar coaster he'd learned about. He listened, although distracted, to John facilitate the meeting and announce the agenda.

He heard himself being introduced, but he had to think of his presentation. He felt he had to nail this in order to honor all the people who had shown him such respect and spent so much time helping to develop him.

Henry stood and began, "I want to thank the committee for inviting me to speak to you today. I am grateful to have the opportunity to share the things I have learned at the feet of several generous and wise leaders over the past several weeks. My name is Henry Williams. I've been with Powell about one and a half years. I work with Paul in industrial client support. I've been lucky enough to receive gifts of advice and guidance since I've worked here."

He turned toward Maria. "Thank you, Maria, for the opportunity to prepare and present this summary." Maria nodded at him and made sure to point out that this presentation was being filmed; so, Henry should stay in the camera's view.

Henry went on, "I have been introduced to many new ideas during my time here. Today, I'd like to leverage The Speed of Trust as a framework for my remarks. The author, Stephen M. R. Covey, who is the son of the 7 Habits Covey, wrote that trust is a combination of competence and character.

He described it using the metaphor of a tree. The roots of the tree are Character represented by intent and integrity. The body of the tree represents Competence. It is made up of capabilities and results. If you ever have the opportunity to read this book, I recommend it."

"It's obvious that some of the lessons I've learned could fall into either category, but let's start with character. Are there any questions before we jump in?" Henry asked as he looked around the room. Seeing no raised hands, he continued. "Character is made up of intent and integrity. Some of the lessons I've learned at Powell about intent include what Paul told me in my first week: be loyal to the firm and embrace the values of it. I have noticed the company has a personality that is contagious. It represents a certain set of values and standard of behavior. Although I never met Mr. Powell myself, I do feel like I understand what kind of a man he was based on how people who represent him act."

Henry said, "Alice taught me the importance of remembering that the way I behave is a reflection of my managers, this site, and the firm. It has meant a lot to me, since I knew I should never do anything to embarrass the Williams name when I was growing up. It has been easy to translate that principle to the workplace. If I think of Powell as my work family, I recognize that everyone around me is equally important to the mission."

Henry continued, "I need to open my eyes and regard all my peers, irrespective of department or job function, as significant contributors to the success of Powell. I can, and should, lend my support to any member of the team. Maria told me about what a kind and generous man Mr. Powell was to every member of his work family. He gave time and attention to all members of the team, regardless of the visibility of their contribution."

Henry paused, lifting a glass to his lips, and taking a sip of the cool water, as he looked around the room. All eyes were on him, and he could see that some had been writing a few notes. After a deep breath, he resumed: "The intent to 'Be Good' as our company motto reminds us, requires us to sometimes take an inventory to see if we are doing the things we should. It can be difficult to identify our blind spots in order to better align ourselves to the company's goals and ideals."

"We should seek and accept feedback", Henry declared. "'Feedback is a gift.' is a statement I remember well from one of my chats with Alice. Just as I wouldn't want someone to avoid telling me my pants were unzipped to avoid embarrassing me," he said, winking at Alice while checking his zipper for comic affect," I would hate to do things wrong for several years without someone telling me I should make a change. I'm glad I've had some people guide me who are more worried about whether I can be successful than whether they might make me uncomfortable with constructive advice."

"The last thing I'll say about intent is 'Don't crap where you eat'." He wasn't sure if this was too pedestrian for this crowd. However, several people nodded slowly, as if they'd already heard this phrase and knew what he meant. He didn't let that get him off course. "There are many things we might do that could create difficult situations for us in the workplace. In some cases, these activities could even disqualify us from certain opportunities. I saw my friend Luke do this. He created for himself a reputation that he couldn't overcome. He'd lost the support of his manager and finally realized his best opportunity was to move on to another firm." He saw Steve looking down as he recalled the experience.

"A reputation is something that must be managed, since a bad reputation is so hard to overcome. I was happy to get pointers early in my career here where I learned that I'd developed a certain reputation. I had to overcompensate for a year before I got advice that I was back on solid ground." Henry could tell he was doing well from the energy in the room when he looked around. They seemed to like what he was saying.

Henry went on, "Let's talk about what I've learned regarding integrity. I've learned about it from a few people. Being responsible for your own career and development are a great starting place. Our society has become more and more entitled. That's why it stands out more and more for someone to own their personal responsibilities.

I trust Paul," Henry said, as he nodded toward Paul. "At the same time, I know that whether I succeed or fail here, get promoted or stagnate, all depends on my own efforts. Paul wants me to succeed; but, he can't force me to do the things I need to do. He can only guide and enable me. Each person must make of their career what they can."

"I want to share with you what I've learned about the research of Angela Duckworth," Henry stated. "Her studies illustrate that success is predictable based on grit, or perseverance. It has a stronger influence than IQ, socioeconomic status, or any other factor. It sounds intuitive; but, she says that the harder one works, the more success they'll have."

It has a lot to do with what Paul taught me about Brene' Brown's work in her book, Daring Greatly. We should be willing to dare to try things even when success isn't assured. Additionally, we need to be willing to overcome disappointment. Things don't always happen according to our wishes; but, our ability to overcome these disappointments is a reflection of our inner core of integrity."

Satisfied that he'd made his point about character, he stopped and looked around the boardroom. He saw Maria had filled two pages of notes. He was interested in what she'd written. As his eyes drifted back across the room, he saw the HR director resting his head in his palm. While Henry wasn't sure what to make of it, he continued speaking.

"Competence is the part of the tree we see in the Trust metaphor," he began again. "Competence is a combination of results and capability. I'm not going to speak about technical skills in my presentation. We all know how rigid Powell's hiring and continuing education programs are. I do want to talk about the things that make us successful in our fields. I was grateful to talk to Dereck, who showed me the value of 'showing up'."

Henry spoke again: "Dereck talked about his own revelation that led him to more fully participate in every meeting as a valued member of mini-committees assigned to meet on specific topics. If the meetings were to be considered true 'group' meetings, then the outcome would be dependent upon everyone showing up."

He wasn't sure he'd explained it well. He paused and looked for signs of confusion on the faces in the boardroom. They seemed to get it; but, to be sure he asked if his point was clear.

"I'd like to clarify one point," Dereck said from the back of the room. "It was John who first asked me to consider why I was selected to attend the meetings and recommended that I contemplate what I could bring to them."

Henry took advantage of the moment when Dereck spoke to take a long, cool drink of water. Looking back at Paul, he could tell Paul approved of the presentation. He was representing Paul well, and his supervisor appeared to be proud of Henry.

"Because I'd developed a bad reputation early on, it took a long time for me to be assigned to any teams," Henry continued. "I knew that while I worked on becoming the kind of associate sponsors would want on their teams, I needed to learn valuable leadership skills. I leveraged the other piece of advice that Dereck gave me. He called it 'Lead where you stand.'"

Alice looked over at Dereck, and they shared a smile. They both remembered that long-ago experience. Dereck had never told Alice her advice had made such a deep impression. Alice was pleased she'd been able to help him.

"To lead where you stand is to exert your influence in your current setting. One does not need a position of leadership to lead," Henry continued. "The best way to show readiness for a leadership role is to demonstrate that you have learned the following traits..." Henry looked around the room as he reached into his pocket for his laser pointer. He pointed at each bullet in his Power Point presentation as he read the traits aloud to the crowd. He paused between each one to watch for any signs of confusion. He could see that Maria had continued taking notes and had captured each of the points he'd made:

- Delegating
- Redirecting conversations to maximize the time spent discussing solutions
- Influencing peers toward a beneficial outcome
- Aligning activities with the priorities of the firm

Seeing that no one seemed to be puzzled, he continued, "Powell's interests are our interests." He remembered saying that at a meeting to discuss the city's interest in Powell's future use of properties for a new school. "When we are able to convey a message in a way that moves others to action, and our motives have the best interest of the firm at their core, we are leading where we stand." He saw several smiles in the room and felt he'd touched a chord with the executives.

He rushed on to his next point: "In order to be known for our results, we must sell ourselves. I remember learning from my parents that we need to be humble and meek. We shouldn't boast about our achievements. That's actually b.s.," Henry said amidst gentle laughter. "Once I learned what Paul and John value, I could be sure to provide those things."

"Lucas is the one who taught me the importance of aligning my goals and motives with my managers. He also taught me to add the extra details that help my manager see the progress of the projects that are important to them," Henry went on. "Lucas also emphasized the importance of correct motives. If we are providing visibility to stakeholders in all activities of a project, we are adding value. This is true whether the assignment shines a light on us, or someone else. If we seek to always shine the light on ourselves, people will see through us; we will possibly be thought of as a sycophant."

BUILD A GREAT CAREER

Henry let the word hang in the air. He knew it was a better word to use than "suck-up"; he was trying to be professional. It appeared that he didn't lose anyone in the room.

Henry turned to smile at his five interviewees. "Again, I want to thank my mentors, official and unofficial: Alice, Paul, Lucas, Dereck, and Maria. Each one of you has been a real source of encouragement and wisdom in my life here at Powell. I feel like you've helped put me on a path where I can continue to build my career, and maybe even help others. Thank you," he said, as he laid his laser pointer on the table.

He stood silently facing the room. There was a sparkle in his eye that Alice and Paul both saw. They were proud of how far Henry had come. The silence was finally broken by Steve. He'd been stoic throughout the meeting; Henry hadn't been able to read him at all. Steve clapped slowly and gave him a look that Henry remembered getting from his father when he'd done something remarkable. He loved this feeling. He knew Steve to be direct and occasionally gruff, so his praise was valuable.

Following Steve's lead, the rest of the room gave Henry a warm round of applause. He felt great.

As the applause began to die down, John stood and walked toward Henry. In his hand he had a small box wrapped in brown paper tied with twine.

John stood right next to Henry, his deep voice booming into the room as he placed his hand on Henry's shoulder, "Henry, we're all so proud of you. We've been talking about you for months and how you have been progressing." Henry about lost it. He couldn't believe that he was a topic of discussion at the highest level at their Powell facility.

John went on, "We are impressed at your ability to accept advice and make changes. This trait is going to continue to serve you well. You showed us today, however, that you do not always have to be fed feedback. You are able to learn from outside sources and integrate information from many resources into your own ideas. Your synthesis of numerous ideas into a set of core principles, organized into such an easy rubric to understand and remember, is outstanding. In your short time here, with the benefit of tutoring, you have developed an understanding of these values that we often learn over the course of many years of leading people." The crowd applauded again. Henry was flush with embarrassment as they clapped. He didn't realize he'd done anything special.

"As you know, Henry," John continued, "Mr. Powell designed a set of coasters that represents many things to this company: concern for details in the representation and care of our clients; our values; and, in this case, recognition of a superior completed project.

An assignment is honored if its scope and contribution is exceptional. Projects are also recognized if they add significantly to the bottom line, or help us achieve more through cultural or technological enhancement. Henry, on behalf of us all, I present you with your own set of the Powell coasters."

John continued, "You see, each time you've been offered a coaster by someone at Powell, it has not been out of a concern for our furniture; although, that is a practical application. The coaster has come to serve as a reminder of what we stand for. I hope that, when you have opportunities to share the coaster with visitors at your desk, you'll remember the lessons you've learned through this project. I also hope you'll remember how you've internalized Powell's mission." Henry stood silently as John handed him the box of coasters. They applauded again. He felt strange standing there in front of the executives with this gift in his hands.

Before he could think much more about it, Maria stood to speak. As the applause died down, Maria asked, "Henry, how do you think you did?" The crowd laughed. There was no need to respond.

Paul and Maria looked at each other and locked eyes briefly when Paul slowly nodded his head. "Henry, we are all impressed at what you have learned. We want to leverage this learning across our facility for every new employee. If we do it well, there is a chance we can export it to our other facilities."

Henry felt great. It was nice to know something he'd worked on could help the company. "I'm happy to help in any way I can," he said. Maria reached out to grasp his hand. "Oh, you will," she said. "We are promoting you to Level 2 and offering you a newly formed position of Emerging Leaders Coordinator. It's a role I've been trying to fill alongside my other responsibilities. We believe you have what it takes to drive this program. What do you think?"

Henry could not believe what was happening. In front of everyone he felt some stress; but, there was no hesitation in accepting the role. He raised the box of coasters high in the air in victory, then shook Maria's hand. He finally took his seat, his head swimming with happiness.

Chapter 13: The New Job

Henry sat in the windowsill of his new office. It was just down the hall from his new boss, Maria, and across the hall from Alice, his mentor. He stared out over the pavement as the flood of cars filed in to take their places. He loved his new job. He had revitalized the emerging leaders program by making some adjustments to the curriculum. He also worked closely with several senior leaders to identify what they look for from a candidate.

He was also asked to provide a portion of the new employee orientation. His presentation was entitled, "What your boss wants you to know, but might not think to tell you." He had presented it a couple of times. It felt like he was adding value to the new employees. He was grateful to have been granted access to some footage of Mr. Powell explaining his mission and vision for the company.

He stood and walked through his door, down the hall, past the break room, and into the classroom where the new hires were waiting for him. "Good morning, I'm Henry Williams. I'll be speaking with you this morning about a few important topics that can make all the difference in your career here at Powell. I've been with the company two years now, and I'm honored to be able to share this information with you. I remember being just like you: bright, fresh, and ambitious. You have a history of success. I'm here to tell you a few of the things your boss wants you to know, but probably won't tell you. First, allow me to show you a video that was recorded by Mr. Powell, our founder..."

Henry pushed play on his screen and dimmed the lights. He was so happy to be sharing the things he'd learned. He'd never expected that he'd be the face of Powell; but, here he was. The young man felt gratitude for the tips he'd received. Henry had taken all the feedback to heart.

Chapter 14:
Summary of Henry's feedback

Tip 1: Observe and embrace the values, and level of professionalism, of your successful co-workers. This includes senior-level staff and those that have influence in the organization.

Tip 2: Accept feedback. It is a gift. It can be difficult for someone to tell you the things they notice in order to help you. Accept feedback and try to understand the root of it. This will help you make the changes needed for improvement.

Tip 3: Be aware of your reputation. Once a reputation is formed, positive or negative, people are predisposed to see you in a certain light. It takes overcompensating to overcome an unfavorable reputation. Good behavior must be consistent and sustained over a long period of time.

People will hook onto any slipup as evidence that no change has occurred. At that point, they'll assume they were right to believe the worst of you all along.

Tip 4: Don't crap where you eat--either in one sudden act or over a series of acts. We crap where we eat when we do something that is serious, public, and career damaging. Such incidents are hard to surmount.

Tip 5: Be responsible for your own development; and, manage your own career. No one has more skin at stake in your future than you. Never wait for others to step up to provide what you should be pursuing on your own.

Tip 6: Strive for grit and perseverance, the strongest predictors of success. They are more important than education, intelligence, or status.

Tip 7: Show up. The ability to simply show up separates you from so many. Being fully engaged and present in all moments is a key to success. Don't underestimate your ability to contribute.

Tip 8: Lead where you stand. A leader is defined not by his role, but by his actions. Leading from within a team is the surest way to show ability to run a team. Leading is having influence. If you care enough about the outcome of a project or activity, you need to direct it so that the outcome is effective.

Tip 9: Be competitive and sell your accomplishments. You may be the smartest person in the organization; yet, a career is built by following your manager's priorities. You must ensure your supervisor has visibility into what you are doing. It's common for effective people to be passed over or ignored simply because the great work they are doing doesn't get any publicity.

If you have a direct supervisor that can help you identify what things you should publicize, leverage that relationship. The supervisor may already be advocating for you. The idea that good work speaks for itself is outdated and patently false.

Tip 10: Be loyal and professional. When you are hired by a firm, or selected by a group, you are also given trust. You represent them. Whatever you do, even outside of work, reflects upon the firm. Your behavior shouldn't be an embarrassment to the company, or to your leaders. If you are sent to a meeting, or to meet with a client, you are representing the company and its management.

Tip 11: Remember customer focus and interdependence. Everyone you work with is part of your network. No one fails or succeeds independently. We all rely on each other for everything necessary to build success in our organizations. While some people are not directly essential to our projects, their contributions are essential to the mission of the company. Treat each member of the team with respect and honor.

Tip 12: Align your goals and behaviors with the needs of the organization. There is great power in keeping things around you that remind you of important principles. Pictures, quotes, or keepsakes can prompt you to be your best.

Tip 13: Remember AARP when trying to overcome an undesirable reputation: <u>A</u>ccept that the information you are hearing is valid; <u>A</u>ssess what information you have been provided; <u>R</u>eject the habits of your old reputation; and, <u>P</u>rotect the reputation you are trying to build.

Tip 14: Dare greatly and accept disappointments graciously. The willingness to attempt a task even though success is not assured is a key attribute of successful people. The risks that come with this kind of living will lead to disappointments. We must have sufficient character to handle disappointment in a professional manner. Our level of maturity influences how we handle setbacks and learn from them.

Tip 15: Know the true foundation of trust. It comes from the combination of competence and character. People trust you and allow you opportunities for these reasons:

- You are competent in your role.

- You have the ability to do what's asked.

- You have a successful track record.

These qualities, combined with confidence in your motives and personal character, build trust. High-trust individuals are able to accomplish more with less effort because they have already proven themselves. Barriers are removed.

Bibliography

Hanford, E. (2012, August). Retrieved from Angela Duckworth and the Research on Grit': http://americanradioworks.publicradio.org/features/tomorrows-college/grit/angela-duckworth-grit.html

Roosevelts, T. (1910). Excerpt from the speech "Citizenship In A Republic". France, Sarbonne.

Recommended Reading

Crucial Accountability, Patterson, Kerry, et. Al.

Daring Greatly, Brown, Brene'

Speed of Trust, Covey, Stephen M. R.

Don't Crap Where you Eat is an allegory about building a great career. All of us have blind spots in our behavior and job performance. We can't see the conduct we need to change or improve. That's why we require others to help us gain perspective. Follow Henry Williams as he overcomes false starts in his career through the gift of feedback from senior team members. See how Henry begins to thrive and leverage the advice to help individuals at the firm and beyond.

About the Author

From the beginning of his career, Bill Ward has been passionate about leadership. He has observed various management styles and researched the topic. This has allowed the author to expand his own influence while helping a variety of people across multiple industries and volunteer organizations. Over the last 20 years, Bill has coached individuals to overcome many common career mistakes. He has also taught other leaders to provide this coaching and mentoring.

Bill's career and interests are varied. He began working in the foodservice industry. However, he has worked in the semiconductor industry for almost twenty years. That is where he has supervised engineers, technicians, programmers, scientists, and other managers. He is active in his church and Toastmasters International.

The author lives in the Washington, D.C., area with his wife, Lauril. They have three daughters and two sons.

www.ingramcontent.com/pod-product-compliance
Lightning Source LLC
Chambersburg PA
CBHW071753170526
45167CB00003B/1010